First published 2010 by
Veritas Publications
7–8 Lower Abbey Street
Dublin 1
Ireland
publications@veritas.ie
www.veritas.ie

ISBN 978 1 84730 222 9

A catalogue record for this book is available from the British Library.

Designed by Kelly Sheridan, Outsource Graphix Ltd, Dublin
Printed in the Republic of Ireland by Walsh Colour Print, Kerry

Veritas books are printed on paper made from the wood pulp of managed forests. For every tree felled, at least one tree is planted, thereby renewing natural resources.

About the Authors

Fiona McAuslan holds a Masters in Mediation and Conflict Resolution Studies from University College Dublin. She is an experienced mediator and conflict coach with many years' experience working with family, workplace and school conflicts. She works in the Irish Family Mediation Service and Clanwilliam Institute and is an accredited Practitioner Mediator with the Mediators Institute of Ireland. Fiona has published the S.A.L.T. Programme: A Conflict Resolution Education Programme for Primary schools. She lives in North County Dublin with her husband, Michael, and two children, Sarah and Ben.

Peter Nicholson is a communications specialist and has built a very successful Marketing and Visual Communications Business over the last fifteen years. Peter and Fiona met whilst working on the S.A.L.T. programme and they have continued to work together on many other projects. He is married to Karen, and they have two children, Patrick and Ailish.

About the Illustrator

Kelly Sheridan studied Classical and Computer Animation in Ballyfermot College of Further Education for three years before attending the Irish Academy of Computer Training (IACT) to study G███████████████████Publishing. A keen illustrator and life drawer, she loves ███████████████████alter Sickert. Originally from Crumlin, Kelly currently live███████████████████Mark.

Read Me First!

This is not just another story book, it's a Tool Book. So what's a Tool Book then? It's a book that explains an issue, shows how children can be affected by it and how they can resolve the problem. It also offers a number of tips and techniques that can be used again and again to improve the ability to deal with Anger on a day-to-day basis.

Section 1
What is Anger?
This is a simple explanation of what Anger is.

Section 2
The Story
The story helps the reader identify Anger in their world and helps open the door to discussing and resolving the issue.

Section 3
Tool Box
The Tool Box has many tips and techniques that can be used in everyday life on an ongoing basis. The more they are practised, the better the result!

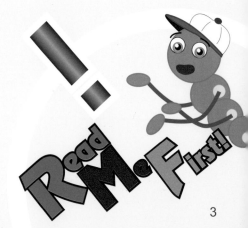

What is Anger?

- Anger is a high-energy emotion.

- Anger is a feeling; it is neither good nor bad.

- We don't always know how best to manage anger.

- Feeling angry is part of being human.

- We can't stop ourselves feeling angry but we can change the way we behave.

Explosive

Exhilerating

Frightening

ANGER

Full of Energy

Hard to Control

Can Change Things
For Better or Worse

What is Anger?

What Triggers Anger?

• Anger comes from our impulse to fight when we think we're in danger.

What Anger Makes Us Feel Like

• The rush of energy means we can act fast.

• Our bodies sweat and tremble and all our muscles tense up.

• We can feel like this all day.

How Does It Happen?

Feelings like fear and frustration trigger a part of our brain called the amygdala *(a-mig-da-la)*. The amygdala floods our brain with adrenalin. This is what makes us feel so angry.

The adrenalin stays in our brain for a long time so we can feel angry all day. It can be hard to calm down and think clearly.

More info VISIT www.resolvingbooks.com/whattriggersanger

Cycle of Anger

Anger Builds
As we think about our hurt, our anger builds.

Thoughts Exaggerate
Our thoughts become more intense.

Anger Strenghtens

We Feel Powerful
In this excited state we feel invincible and powerful, and that gives us a feeling of security.

We Want Revenge
We get to a state where forgiveness is out of the question and revenge becomes the only thing on our minds.

We Convince Ourselves We Are Right
We become convinced in our views and sure that we are right. This stream of angry thoughts helps us to feel justified in ourselves. They become the reason for our continued rage.

And Anger Builds ...

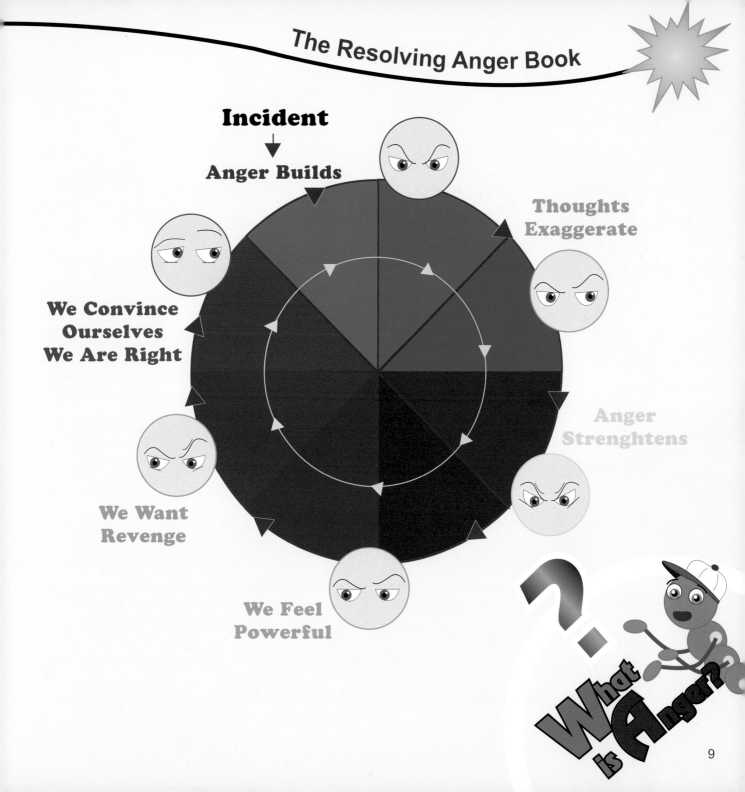

Incident

Anger Builds

Thoughts
Exaggerate

We Convince
Ourselves
We Are Right

Anger
Strenghtens

We Want
Revenge

We Feel
Powerful

What is Anger?

9

Jack likes to climb and he likes to run.

Jack is quick to make up his mind.
When he gets angry he explodes.

Jack will fight. He is not scared of anything.

Jack decides to make a kennel for his dog, Boots.

This is Sam.

Jack and Sam are friends.

Sam decided to help Jack build Boots' kennel,
and they both got started.

In no time at all they had the kennel nearly built.

When Jack gets angry, his head fills with hotness.

Jack wanted to hit someone and he wanted his own way.

He wanted to be right and he wanted to win.

When Sam gets angry he digs his heels in. He doesn't get angry; he just says no! Nobody tells Sam what to do.

Jack's head got hotter and hotter.

Then, he exploded.

Jack pushed Sam hard.

Curly asked Jack what had happened but Jack didn't want to talk. He was too angry.

He shouted at Curly to go away.

Curly pressed further. He told Jack that he wanted to understand.

How angry are you?

Are you... not angry... this angry... or this angry?

Cool

Hot

Boiling

Very angry then!
Sam made me so mad I wanted to hit him!
It was my idea to paint.

Was the brush important?
I wanted to do the painting and Sam wouldn't give me the brush. He wanted to paint.
TAXI
TO DO:
JACK

Jack thought for a minute.

He didn't know the answer to that.
Nobody had won.

Curly found him sitting outside, looking rather annoyed.

Sam held tightly onto the brush. He wasn't letting go of it.

Curly asked Sam what he was going to paint.

I like Jack, but he can be bossy...
but maybe he doesn't know that, and I didn't try to tell him because I was too busy being angry myself.
Seems to me like you missed a good chance to tell him, but there is another way, you know... come with me.

Jack and Sam watched the computer screen.

Look what you guys could have done.

Onscreen, Jack was hammering away while Sam cut up some wood.

'This is going to be great,' said Jack onscreen.

'Yes, we'll be finished soon,' agreed Sam.

Let's talk about 'The Anger Rules'.

It's ok to feel angry but...

1. Don't hurt others.
2. Don't hurt yourself.
3. Don't damage property.
4. Talk about it.

Stay Cool!

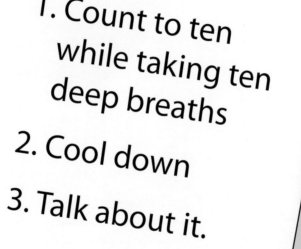

What to do:

1. Count to ten while taking ten deep breaths

2. Cool down

3. Talk about it.

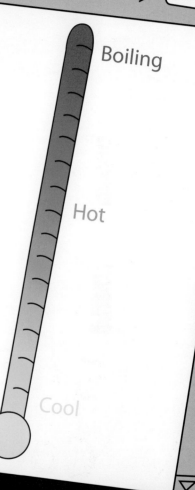

Boiling

Hot

Cool

10

9

8

7

6

Inhale
slowly

Jack and Sam watched the screen carefully.

'I'm angry because you won't give me the brush,' said Jack onscreen.

'Jack, I said I wanted to paint. I won't give you the brush,' replied Sam onscreen.

Now Sam has to stop and think about what to say.

I WANT TO PAINT!
I DON'T LIKE BEING TOLD WHAT TO DO!
I suppose... it's his dog.
WHY SHOULD HE GET ALL THE COOL JOBS?
Would Jack listen to me?
I could just say no... but then what?

STOP and ask yourself:

1. Why are you feeling angry?

2. Can you put it into words?

Remember...

1. Only speak on behalf of yourself.

2. Try and start with 'I'
   (I think, I feel).

3. Be honest but not unkind.

Boots' kennel looked great. Jack and Sam were friends again. Everyone was happy.

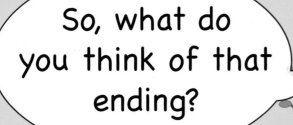

Remember:

1. If you are angry, take ten deep breaths and cool down.

2. Speak from your own point of view.

3. Listen to what the other person is saying.
   It will help you and them to sort things out.

4. Talk about how you really feel.
   Don't be unkind, be honest.

5. Use the 'I' statement (I think, I feel).

6. Use the Working Together Maze (at the end of this book)
   to help problem-solve.

7. We can all be winners!

The Caterpillar

- The Caterpillar in the story plays the part of a mediator. The questions he asks and the way he listens are all done using mediation skills.

- A mediator does not judge people or take sides. Their role is to use their skills to help people resolve their own conflict. They do this by listening to each person, asking questions and using negotiation techniques to help the person think and learn about what they are feeling.

- The mediator helps them to talk to each other and to understand each other's point of view. In doing so, they can find a way forward together.

Stays Cool

Helps Find Solutions

Remains Impartial

Understands

Doesn't Judge

Asks Good Questions

Tool Box

The Caterpillar Helped Because...

Listening helps calm kids.

Listening helps kids work things out for themselves.

Good questions help kids talk about what really bothers them.

Focusing on them helps kids think about their own thoughts and feelings.

Helping kids sort it out for themselves helps them learn to be better friends.

Skills used by the Caterpillar in this story:

1. **Listening** to what Jack and Sam felt and why they got angry with each other is a more effective way of helping them learn from their row. If they were simply told to behave, they would not have had the opportunity to learn about what made them angry and how to handle this emotion better in the future. When Jack felt listened to, he was more willing to face the possibility of changing the way he got angry. When Sam felt listened to, he opened up and talked about what was really bothering him. It helped both of them to improve their friendship.

2. The **questions** the Caterpillar asks help Jack and Sam talk about what really bothers them and makes a big difference in how they understand the real nature of their row.

3. The Caterpillar does not talk about himself. **He concentrates on Jack and Sam.** This means they have to focus on their own thoughts and feelings.

4. The Caterpillar helps the boys **sort out the problem themselves** without making his own suggestions. The boys learn more from doing it their way. This means the solution they come to is one they can keep and as a result they become better friends.

All the skills and ideas that the Caterpillar uses can be used by anyone reading this story to help them in their own lives.

Measuring Anger

- What colour do you think of when you are really angry?

- What colour do you think of when you are cool?

- What colours go in between?

Boiling

Hot

Cool

Draw your own thermometer

1. Colour it in.

2. What colour do you think of when you get really angry?

When we get angry our brain stops thinking. We find it hard to know what is happening to us. The thermometer can help us to learn about ourselves.

When you get angry you can use your thermometer to ask:

1. How hot did you get?

2. What happened?

3. Who did you show your anger to?

4. How did you feel inside?

5. What did you do?

6. What made you angry?

7. What did you do to get control of your anger?

8. Did you direct your anger, repress it (squash it) or explode?

Anger Rules

Anger is an emotion. It is alright to feel angry. We can learn how to handle it better. We need to be able to talk about how we feel but also know what behaviour to avoid.

When you are talking about anger, use the 'I' statement (I think, I feel)

1. Don't hurt others.

2. Don't hurt yourself.

3. Don't damage property.

4. Talk about it.

What to do:

Do think and plan what strategies will work for you when you are angry while you are calm and can think clearly.

Don't wait until you are in the heat of the situation before deciding how to manage your anger.

Do take time to cool down. Recognise that you need time for your anger to pass. Breathe deeply, count backwards from 10, or 20, or 30, or even 100!

Don't let your anger carry on building unchecked.

Do stop and think, 'What will the consequences be of any action I take now?'

Don't forget that what you do now will have consequences for you later.

Do take some time out to compose yourself.

Don't face the person until you have gained control of yourself.

Do distract yourself with something else. Go out and play; watch a fun film; read a magazine or book. Visualise a place or hum a song that you like.

Don't dwell on your angry thoughts. That will only make you angrier.

Do remember that there are two sides to every story.

Don't demonise the other person.

Do use the following phrase types (*for example*):

I feel…	I feel really angry
When…	when you lie about me
I would like…	I would like you to stop

Cooling Down

Breathing deeply and counting backwards from 10 can help you cool down before deciding what to do.

Counting backwards from 10, or even 20, helps our brain calm down and start to think again.

The adrenalin subsides and we can start talking more calmly about what has annoyed us.

Remember:
Our brain can stay in a heightened state for a number of hours after it has been triggered, even when we feel calmer. It is important to take a few minutes to cool down whenever you feel your anger building again.

Cool Down Checklist ☑

- Stop - take some long, deep breaths.

- Count slowly from 10 - 1.

- Breathe in through your nose and out through your mouth.

- Remember to think cool thoughts and not hot thoughts *(see the next page)*.

- Think of a happy place where you feel safe.

- Imagine a balloon filling with your anger and then deflating, releasing your anger.

- Find a pattern in the room (on the carpet, wall paper) and trace around it with your eyes.

- Go and write down why you are angry.

- Go for a walk.

- Hug a large cushion.

When you have calmed down, you are ready to solve the problem.

When we start to get angry and we can feel ourselves losing it, remember the Cool Down Checklist.

The more you use it, the more you will find it useful. It works because it helps our brain cool down and start to think again.

Why not...

Make your own checklist

Download a template from www.resolvingbooks.com

Read this book

...next time you feel angry.

Hot and Cool Thoughts

When we get angry we often start saying negative things to ourselves. This can make us angrier.

We need to change those thoughts to good thoughts to help us cool down. If we can do this we can make a significant difference to our situation.

Think about it...
Talk about it...

1. What hot thoughts do you get when you're angry?

2. When you say them out loud, how does it make you feel?

3. Now look at the cool thoughts. Try saying them out loud instead.

4. The next time you're angry, try and remember the cool thoughts list. Change that hot thought into a cool thought.

5. It's hard to begin with, but keep practising. Remember that we can change the way we react to anger... but it takes time.

You make me sick

I need to think about what to do

Nobody likes me

I'll talk to my friends

I'll get back at them!

Things will look better in the morning

It's not fair!

Let it go!

Tool Box

What People See on the Outside

Our bodies can tell us a lot about how we feel. We can tell how people are feeling by looking at their faces and bodies. It is important to understand these signals.

Can you tell which of these 8 bodies are angry?

Conflict Iceberg

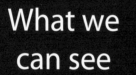

What we can see

What we can't see

Sometimes we don't say what we mean. We are like icebergs - most of what we think and feel is under the surface.

Here are some good questions to ask to help someone talk about how they really feel:

1. What happened?

2. What did you do?

3. What do you think about what happened?

4. How did you feel?

5. How are you now?

6. What do you think should happen next?

7. What do you want to do?

How People Feel on the Inside

When we get angry it can be like a body alarm going off. The adrenalin that floods our brain affects our whole body.

Here are some signs to look for:

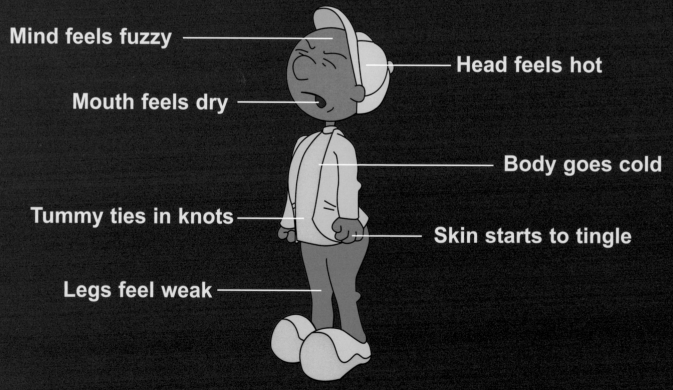

Mind feels fuzzy

Head feels hot

Mouth feels dry

Body goes cold

Tummy ties in knots

Skin starts to tingle

Legs feel weak

Which ones do you feel?

Remember, these are natural body reactions. Don't be frightened.

The next time you feel your body alarm going off:

1. Take slow, deep breaths.

2. Feel the adrenalin run through your body. Remember it will flow away again.

3. Take time out. Go for a walk, count down from ten...

4. Wait until you are calm before speaking.

Working Together

1. **STOP AND THINK:** Are you ready to work things out?

2. **ASK:** What do each of you want to happen?

3. **LISTEN** to what the other person wants to happen. Then, in your own words, write down what the other person wants to happen.

4. **TALK:** Now that you know what the other person wants, you can write a list of all the things you need to agree on together.

5. **TALK:** Choose one of the issues on the list and think of ideas that might help you solve it. Don't worry if they sound strange or silly. Include everything; the bigger the list, the better. This is called 'brainstorming'.

6. **TALK:** Now each of you circle the three ideas you like best. Then each of you crosses out the three you like least.

7. **CHOOSE** the ones that you both agree on and talk about them some more. If you have not circled any that are the same, then circle your next choice.

8. When you have agreed on your choice, write down your agreement here under 'Number 1'.

Now go back and brainstorm the next issue.

Learning from our Mistakes

There is no doubt that there will be times when we get angry and don't remember to behave well... even after reading this book!

It is possible to learn from these times. Thinking about what happened can help us learn for the future.

Think about the time you got angry.
Do any of these statements apply:

1. I should have calmed down by using the Checklist *(p. 74)*.

2. I should have thought cool thoughts and not hot thoughts *(p. 76)*.

3. I should have waited until I cooled down before I said what I thought.

4. I need to remember the Anger Rules *(p. 70)*.

What I will do next time:

1. I will cool down before I speak.

2. I will remember to ask the other person: 'What do you think?'

3. I will choose my battles.

4. I will remember that nothing is worth hurting myself or other people.

Rehearsal Room

Tool Box